The Mary Mind

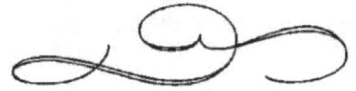

©John Mark Lucas
All rights reserved. This book or any portion thereof may not be reproduced or used in any manner whatsoever without the express written permission of the authors.

First printing: 2017
ISBN 978-0-692-98940-1
John Mark Lucas/Fourth Chakra House
PO Box 25231
Winston-Salem, NC 27114
contact@fourthchakrahouse.com
www.themarymind.com

Cover art: The Annunciation, by Henry Ossawa Tanner
American (active France), 1859 – 1937
Philadelphia Museum of Art

Interior illustrations: Gustave Doré, French, 1832-1883

Ordering information:
The Mary Mind is available online at www.themarymind.com

The Mary Mind

John Mark Lucas and Rev. Elizabeth Forrest

Fourth Chakra House

Table of Contents

Prelude... i
Peace and Love... 1
The Mary Mind... 5
The Joseph Mind...................................... 10
We Are All Joseph. We Are All Mary............ 15
The Christ Consciousness is Born................. 17
Shepherds and Wise Men........................... 20
The New Thought Meets the Old.................. 28
The Missing Years.................................... 32
Hard Times Are Bound to Come.................. 34
The Apostles... 39
It's a Miracle!... 43
Turning Water Into Wine........................... 44
Raising Lazarus from the Dead.................... 50
Healing 10 Lepers.................................... 59
Feeding the 5000..................................... 64
Walking on Water and Calming the Sea......... 68
Crucifixion and Resurrection...................... 73
Benediction.. 79

Prelude

Storytelling is an art. Great stories and parables, like the ones that are passed down through generations and cultures, always teach us something, usually about ourselves.

With that in mind, we would like to invite you to settle in while we tell you a few stories, or parables. They were written long ago and have been rewritten and reinterpreted many times. The stories come from a book that is all about a super hero from another time. The book is wildly popular. In fact, it's been a best seller for years. The book is the Bible.

There are a lot of similarities between Bible stories and other kinds of stories – fairytales for instance. Many versions of the Bible start off with something like, "In the beginning," while many fairytales start off with something like, "Once upon a time." It's really the same thing, just different words to get the plot going.

Like all parables, Bible stories have meanings, morals and messages. Depending on who is telling the story and what their point of view or motive is, those meanings, morals and messages can vary greatly. The co-authors of this book also have a point of view about the Bible, its stories, and most importantly, what it teaches us about Jesus and how to live our lives.

We also have a sense of humor. So we hope you'll smile a little as your read this book.

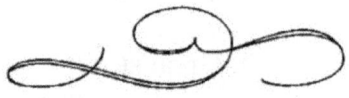

We see Jesus as a great mystic teacher. He was a man who became an awakened Master in his day and invited others to follow his path if they wanted to find the same enlightenment, or divinity, that he found through Peace and Love, or God.

We see Mary, the mother of Jesus, as a great mystic mind. Her acceptance and willingness to be filled with the Christ Consciousness is our example of giving your life to Peace and Love, or God.

We see the gospels, Matthew, Mark, Luke and John, as great mystic texts. They use the poetic language of parables to tell the story of Jesus and Mary, and to deliver the message of Peace and Love, or God.

Reverend Elizabeth Forrest
John Mark Lucas

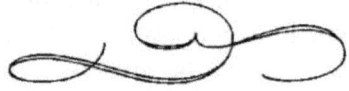

Peace and Love

Jesus was a storyteller. To express his ideas he told parables, which was a popular way of teaching in his day. Parables use situations, ideas and events in one way to make a point in another way. They have a tendency to simplify larger concepts or meanings so people can identify with the circumstances of the story while still getting the bigger picture. This method of teaching makes the stories more relatable to the reader or listener.

When we look at the parables Jesus used and what he taught, we do not see a religious zealot. He issues no threat of eternal damnation and makes no claim of superiority or being holier than the rest of us. No, Jesus was a brother, a spiritual mentor to the people who followed him. And as you'll see, he taught only two things. He taught only *Peace and Love*.

The *Love* that Jesus taught was not the emotional love that one person may feel for another. That kind of love is always nice, but it is not the Love that he was talking about. What Jesus called Love was not about *us*, it was about *God*. The Bible makes that connection between God and Love very clear, and in I John we see that *Love is actually another name for God.*

> I John 4:16, NKJV
>
> *"God is love; and he that dwells in love dwells in God, and God in him."*

Simply put: To be Godly is to be Loving. To be Loving is to be Godly. It will be important to remember that the words "God" and "Love" are interchangeable in this book.

The *Peace* that Jesus taught was not a truce between nations or some kind of "rest in peace" that you wind down into after your body dies. The Peace he was talking about is a *state of mind* − a way of thinking that is not at war with yourself, others or the world around you. Peace is a mind that is free of conflict and interacts with the world in Loving, or Godly ways. Jesus was, and is, teaching us how to live our everyday lives so we can experience Peace of Mind, or better, the Mind of Peace.

The story of Jesus has been almost hopelessly hijacked. By turning him into a religious figure to be worshiped, we've lost him as the spiritual teacher that he actually was. He is presented as the one and only Son of God, the King of Kings, a Miracle Worker, a Boy Wonder. His message of Peace and Love has been shoved aside and replaced with a theology of idol worship.

This is so unfortunate. Religions built up around Jesus present us with a doctrine of fear and intimidation, threatening us with eternal damnation unless we:

- Fear God
- Accept that we are sinners
- Believe that only Jesus can save us from our sins

These are man-made ideas that twist and distort the story of Jesus so it becomes a tactic to control people, empower governments and sustain churches. If that sounds harsh to you, we want you to know that we are not here to argue against traditional teachings. Honest. We are not here to convert. We simply want to look at some of the Bible's stories through the lens of Peace and Love.

In the four gospels we have the story of Jesus. But behind that story, hiding in plain sight, there is a treasure waiting for us. That treasure is not diamonds, rubies or pearls, but something more precious.

That treasure is the enlightenment that leads to the Christ Consciousness of Peace and Love, or God.

Do you want to discover that treasure? If so, we believe the story of Jesus can show you how to find it. The purpose of *The Mary Mind* is to walk with you toward that treasure by offering you a new way to think about some old stories.

The Mary Mind

When Mary says "Yes" she becomes the first real disciple of Jesus, or the Christ Consciousness.

What would you do if a crazy-looking fortune teller appeared out of nowhere and told you something so unbelievable, so out-of-this-world that there was no way it could be true? For example, what if this gypsy told you that starting tomorrow all the dogs in the neighborhood would no longer bark. Instead, they would start talking, just like you.

Oh, but wait, there's more. We forgot to mention that the fortune teller who gave you this news was actually not even a real person. She was an angel. Like with wings. And as a bonus, the angel said she was sent from God who wanted you to have this information because he mightily favored you. In other words, The Almighty just really, really likes you.

To most of us that would be bananas. But there would also be, somewhere in the world, a person or two who would embrace that message. Someone who might think, "I don't know how in the world dogs will be able to speak, but my-oh-my, won't that be fun!"

This person, this open-minded soul, is able to suspend their human thinking and contemplate an idea that seems impossible in everyday life. Without knowing the "how" of dogs being able to talk, this person says "Yes" to the possibility of it happening and is excited about sitting down with the Chihuahua next door and getting the latest news from the corner fire hydrant.

Well, this is how the Bible story of Jesus begins. Not with talking dogs, but with a story just as incredible. A young girl is visited by an angel who tells her that she is going to give birth to a child who will become the savior of the world. And as if that's not enough, the kicker is that she will become pregnant before she ever marries and "knows" her future husband. One more thing: the father of her baby is going to be God.

Much like hearing that dogs are going to start talking, this, "I'm a pregnant virgin and the baby's daddy is God," business would be hard for most of us to swallow. And forget about the whole angel part. That just makes it supernaturally unbelievable. But in this Bible story, we are introduced to an extraordinary young girl whose name is Mary.

> Luke 1:26–38, NKJV
>
> *^{26} Now in the sixth month the angel Gabriel was sent by God to a city of Galilee named Nazareth, ^{27} to a virgin betrothed to a man whose name was Joseph, of the house of David. The virgin's name was Mary. ^{28} And having come in, the angel said to her, "Rejoice, highly favored one, the Lord is with you; blessed are you among women!"*
>
> *^{29} But when she saw him, she was troubled at his saying, and considered what manner of greeting this was. ^{30} Then the angel said to her, "Do not be afraid, Mary, for you have found favor with God. ^{31} And behold, you will conceive in your womb and bring forth a Son, and shall call His name Jesus. ^{32} He will be great, and will be called the Son of the Highest; and the Lord God will give Him the throne of His father David. ^{33} And He will reign over the*

> *house of Jacob forever, and of His kingdom there will be no end."*
>
> *^{34}Then Mary said to the angel, "How can this be, since I do not know a man?" ^{35}And the angel answered and said to her, "The Holy Spirit will come upon you, and the power of the Highest will overshadow you; therefore, also, that Holy One who is to be born will be called the Son of God. ^{36}Now indeed, Elizabeth your relative has also conceived a son in her old age; and this is now the sixth month for her who was called barren. ^{37}For with God nothing will be impossible."*
>
> *^{38}Then Mary said, "Behold the maidservant of the Lord! Let it be to me according to your word." And the angel departed from her.*

This is what's called the Annunciation. A celebrated event, feast and ceremony for Christians around the world, the Annunciation basically starts off the story of Jesus in the New Testament and pretty much solidifies Mary's place as a player in Christianity. And while it's nice that the church today recognizes Mary as a saint, it seems like after the birth of Jesus, the Bible gently moved her into the background and she became a secondary character. Mary did her business of giving birth to Jesus, but then the story steers away from her, downgrading the immaculately conceived virgin who gave birth to the savior of the world into a supporting role.

In this book, we are going to restore Mary to top billing *along with* Jesus in the greatest story ever told. What's more, she will be our role model, the ideal or example we can look to when we are seeking to grow spiritually.

She is our mystic guide, the embodiment of enlightenment.

When we look at the story of the Annunciation, it can be seen as more than a special news bulletin that interrupts Mary's regularly scheduled programming. It's a moment when time slips off the clock and slides to the floor. Something extraordinary is happening that defies time and space. This is where Mary meets her destiny.

But as Mary is taking all this in, just before she steps onto the world stage, the scripture tells us she is troubled.

> [28] *And having come in, the angel said to her, "Rejoice, highly favored one, the Lord is with you; blessed are you among women!"* [29] *But when she saw him, she was troubled at his saying, and considered what manner of greeting this was.*

What's troubling Mary? Is it the fact that an angel has flown into her house? Somehow, that doesn't really seem to rattle her. The passage says she is troubled by the angel's manner of greeting, *"Rejoice, highly favored one, the Lord is with you; blessed are you among women!"* Mary is not troubled by *how* an angel has appeared, she's just unsure about *why* there's an angel in the room.

Gabriel, being a good angel, calms her down and says, *"Do not be afraid, Mary, for you have found favor with God."* Then he breaks the news to her about being pregnant. Her response? Just one question, *"How shall this be, seeing how I know not a man?"* The angel answers her with an explanation that would probably not have satisfied many of us, *"The Holy Spirit will come upon you, and the power of the Highest will overshadow you."*

The Mary Mind

It's right here, when most of us would have been unable to accept such an answer, that Mary lets go of her "troubles" or doubts. Her mind expands and she embraces the angel's message. Mary says, *"Behold the maidservant of the Lord! Let it be to me according to your word."*

In other words, Mary says, *"Yes."*

This is one of the most moving moments in the Bible. When Mary says, "Yes," she becomes the first real disciple of Jesus, or the Christ Consciousness. Mary's "Yes" is her spiritual awakening to *Truth,* her mind being set free from the contamination of proof.

In the Annunciation parable, the birth of the Christ Consciousness happens when a young girl comes face to face with the Light. Instead of being frightened or backing away from the experience, she steps into the revelation of the moment and the message of its Truth. The Light, or Holy Spirit, overshadows the troubled human mind that says, "No," and gives birth to the illuminated mind that says, "Yes."

Mary's enlightened mind has been right in front of us for centuries. Paintings, frescos, drawings and even pottery have depicted the mother of Jesus surrounded by the Light. In artistic language this Light is seen as a halo that encircles her head. The halo is our visual clue that Mary's mind is illuminated.

In this book our role model will be Mary. If you can follow her example of saying *"Yes"* to the Christ Consciousness, your own blazing halo will illuminate a new mind in you that will start to remove the blocks to Love, or God.

This new mind is *The Mary Mind.*

The Joseph Mind

*Joseph is us, a fact-focused,
proof-needing kind of person.*

There is of course someone else to consider when it comes to Mary's pregnancy. That would be Joseph. He is the very human side of this supernatural story.

Matthew 1:18-19, NKJV

> *[18] Now the birth of Jesus Christ was as follows: After His mother Mary was betrothed to Joseph, before they came together, she was found with child of the Holy Spirit. [19] Then Joseph her husband, being a just man, and not wanting to make her a public example, was minded to put her away secretly.*

Here is a man whose life must have been turned upside-down and inside-out by an event that he had nothing to do with. Mary, his betrothed, had gone away for several months and when she got back to town she had some big news for Joseph.

- She says she's pregnant
- She says she's still a virgin
- She says the father of her child is God

You can bet this must have been a very difficult conversation between Mary and Joseph. Mary knew the *Truth* of the situation but Joseph could only see the *facts*, and it was clearly the facts that Joseph believed when he decided to, *"put her away secretly."*

The Mary Mind

In those days, an engagement was basically considered a legal agreement. If an engagement was called off, it required a divorce even though the official marriage had not taken place. Or, if there had been adultery, stoning the woman was an option. So when the scripture says that Joseph decided to, *"put her away secretly,"* it's indicating he was going to divorce Mary, which would have been a secret or private matter, as opposed to a stoning, which would have been a public matter.

Now, if you're shocked at the idea of Joseph and Mary being on the verge of divorce, just hold on. We know it sounds like we're heathens but trust us, we are not. This idea of Joseph divorcing Mary actually makes him more real. Joseph is *us,* a fact-focused, proof-needing kind of person. Mary is the ideal, but dear, sweet, human Joseph is our "Everyman." He is someone we can identify with, a person with very human reactions.

Obviously, Joseph didn't follow through with the divorce. Why not? What did he do that changed his mind? When we look at the first chapter of Matthew, we see that he did the most human thing possible. He took a nap.

>Matthew 1:20
>
>*[20] But while he thought about these things, behold, an angel of the Lord appeared to him **in a dream**, saying, "Joseph, son of David, do not be afraid to take to you Mary your wife, for that which is conceived in her is of the Holy Spirit.*

With circumstances as they were, you can imagine that Joseph had a lot to think about. So, it looks like he went to bed to mull things over. Does this sound familiar? Haven't we all been advised to not make an important decision until we've, "slept on it"?

It's during his sleep that Joseph is visited by an angel who advises him to go ahead and take Mary as his wife. The angel confirms the incredible story about the pregnancy and assures the jittery bridegroom that marrying her is the right thing to do. So, it's a nap and an angel that changed Joseph's mind.

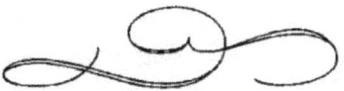

Joseph continues to get his best information while he's asleep. In the book of Matthew, it says he had three more angelic dreams, each one with an important message that saves Jesus' life.

> Joseph is told to go to Egypt to escape King Herod.
> Matthew 2:14, NKJV

*¹³Now when they [the wise men] had departed, an angel of the Lord appeared to Joseph **in a dream**, saying, "Arise, take the young Child and His mother, flee to Egypt, and stay there until I bring you word; for Herod will seek the young Child to destroy Him." ¹⁴ When he arose, he took the young Child and His mother by night and departed for Egypt.*

> Joseph is told to go to Israel.
> Matthew 2:19-21, NKJV

*¹⁹ Now when Herod was dead, behold, an angel of the Lord appeared **in a dream** to Joseph in Egypt,*

The Mary Mind

> [20] *saying, "Arise, take the young Child and His mother, and go to the land of Israel, for those who sought the young Child's life are dead."* [21] *Then he arose, took the young Child and His mother, and came into the land of Israel.*

Joseph is directed to go to Galilee.
Matthew 2:22, NKJV

> [22] *But when he heard that Archelaus was reigning over Judea instead of his father Herod, he was afraid to go there. And being warned by God **in a dream**, he turned aside into the region of Galilee.*

When we look at Joseph's situation as a parable, we can see that his "dreams" are another way of saying that he had to be in an "altered state" to hear from God. Don't most of us also have to do that? Only we might call it meditation, prayer, walking a labyrinth, chanting, saying the rosary or some other practice that leaves us open to intuition, revelation or having a conversation with God.

Mary needed no altered state. She was a pure, clear communication channel. But Joseph had to work at it. He needed to take himself into a quiet space in order to hear himself think. He has the very human *Joseph Mind*.

Who do you identify with, Joseph or Mary? It seems like most of us are like Joseph. Our roots run deep into the hard ground of humanness instead of the fertile soil of the spirit. However, this doesn't mean we are totally cut off from angelic messengers as we go through our day. We've all been inspired while taking a shower, driving to work or just as we're falling asleep or waking up. But when that happens, we usually don't think of it as a visitation by an angel. We call it a bright idea, flash of insight, inner voice or a thousand other names. Over the centuries, the words have changed but the meaning remains the same.

There's no denying that some of the voices in our head are definitely not divine messages. Just look at history and all the hurt, destruction, war and ruin we have brought upon ourselves in the name of a god or spiritual ideal or leader. The list is long and sad. And it continues today.

The questions then become, "How do we quiet The Joseph Mind that listens to all the reasons Love is not the answer on both the personal and global levels?" and, "How do we nurture The Mary Mind that breaks us wide open to hear the voice for Peace and Love?"

That's where Jesus comes in.

The Mary Mind

We Are All Joseph. We Are All Mary.

Jesus is here to teach us how to move the dial from The Joseph Mind to The Mary Mind.

The Joseph Mind and The Mary Mind are like two radio stations playing at the same time. They each have their own playlists and they broadcast 24-hours-a-day, seven-days-a-week. Forever. And you can never turn them off. Ever.

It's impossible to not be listening to one or the other. You can switch the channels back and forth but you're always listening to something. And while you may hear only one station at a time, that doesn't mean the other one isn't on the air.

Most of us are tuned into The Joseph Mind station. That's the one powered by our ego, our attachments and our need to create order and rules to protect our fragile sense of self and shifting beliefs. To change that station we have to go into a quiet place, or an "altered state" to find the controls. The good news is that even though we may be listening to The Joseph Mind station, The Mary Mind station is playing and patiently waiting to be heard. Jesus is here to teach us how to move the dial from The Joseph Mind to The Mary Mind.

These two stations, these two minds – the spirit and the ego, the yin and the yang, the earth and sky, God and man – are in each of us. Spiritual teachings old and new have called these two opposites different names, but they are all talking about the same thing. They are two halves of the one whole. One is the rigid, physically-oriented, *fact-based* mind, and the other is the flexible, spiritually-oriented, *Truth-based* mind.

At this point, we want to ask you a question. Are you willing to try and let go of your preconceived ideas about Jesus? Can you let go of the idea he is a figure you are supposed to worship as the Almighty Savior or else be thrown into hell? Would you be open to letting that idea go, even if it's just while you're reading this book?

If so, we want to introduce you to a Jesus whose sole purpose is to demonstrate and teach Peace and Love. He doesn't want authority over your soul. He's mystic, not maniacal. He is a man who discovered "the secret" to life that so many of us are seeking.

You may be disappointed, but that secret isn't about manifesting wealth or perfect relationships or health. It's also not about going to church and praying to a poor man nailed to a cross. The history surrounding those ideas is both fanciful and horrific, but they have nothing to do with the Jesus in this book.

Jesus was a man who became a spiritual Master during his life. Tragically, his story has been rewritten from one of enlightenment to one of overlord. *The Mary Mind* wants to put the Light back into his story and give you a new way to look at your own story.

The Christ Consciousness is Born

This birth is happening al fresco and au naturale.

The story of Jesus can be read as a parable of spiritual awakening told through the life of a man who walked the earth, became enlightened and awakened to the Christ Consciousness of Love. All the events in his life can be seen as lessons to live by so that each one of *us* can awaken just as Jesus did. So loosen your grip on any traditional religious concepts or dogma you may have about him. We're not asking you to give any of that up, we're just inviting you to look at the birth, life and death of Jesus in a new way.

The Biblical telling of the birth of Jesus is a very sweet comforting story, almost like a lullaby. An innocent baby being born in a manger with cattle lowing, shepherds on their knees, wise men on camels bearing gifts and overhead, a bright star illuminating the scene. It's the perfect setting for a messiah's birth and the meaning of the Christmas story.

Many of us have precious memories around Christmas and this story. As we've said, we're not here to contradict anything you hold dear in your heart. We love Christmas too, and feel it's a very special time to remember Jesus and his message of Peace and Love.

But we also believe this beautiful story is about more than the birth of a very special child – a child conceived by the Virgin Mary, fathered by God, and then delivered into the world in a special way.

The Mary Mind

As the story goes, there was, "no room in the inn," and Joseph and Mary ended up in a stable or barn, or as some scholars have said, they took shelter in a cave. The point is, Jesus was born in a non-traditional physical structure surrounded by nature. So right at the very beginning of the Jesus story, all the usual conditions of a "worldly" birth are missing. There's no hospital, nurse, doctor, midwife or sterile environment. This birth is happening *al fresco* and *au naturale*.

Why would the story of Jesus start out this way? Why would a king or savior of the world be born outside or in seemingly deprived circumstances? Forget about ideas like no room at the inn. Go deeper.

Remember, this book is about the transformation of The Joseph Mind into The Mary Mind, or the mind of man into the mind of Peace. So with that mental framework, we ask you to consider that the birth of Jesus is not really about the birth of a child, but rather about the birth of enlightenment, or the Christ Consciousness, and the very heart of our journey to The Mary Mind.

The reason the "Christ" is delivered outside, literally and metaphorically, the confines of the traditional human experience is really pretty simple, just like most spiritual Truths. Jesus' birth story is telling us that the Christ Consciousness waiting to be born in each of us is a *natural event*, but not a *human event*. The Christ Consciousness isn't a part of the man-made world. In fact, the man-made world is the distracting chatter that keeps us in The Joseph Mind and cut off from the kind of thinking that moves us into The Mary Mind. In today's terms, this outside birth is reminding us to think outside the box.

Shepherds and Wise Men

*The weight of the baggage we carry
determines the length of our journey.*

Let's think about the characters who show up at the beginning of Jesus' life – the shepherds and the wise men. Here are two groups of people who don't seem to have much in common. On one side you have poor laborers and on the other side you have very wealthy men.

Have you ever wondered why these people, those having little and those who seem to have everything, are the only ones who are specifically written about as having journeyed to meet Jesus? Let's think about that.

The story of the shepherds is told in Luke and the wise men's journey is found in Matthew.

> Luke 2:8-16, NKJV
>
> *[8] Now there were in the same country shepherds living out in the fields, keeping watch over their flock by night. [9] And behold, an angel of the Lord stood before them, and the glory of the Lord shone around them, and they were greatly afraid. [10] Then the angel said to them, "Do not be afraid, for behold, I bring you good tidings of great joy which will be to all people. [11] For there is born to you this day in the city of David a Savior, who is Christ the Lord. [12] And this will be the sign to you: You will find a Babe wrapped in swaddling cloths, lying in a manger." [13] And suddenly there was with the angel a multitude of the heavenly host praising God and saying: [14] "Glory to God in the highest, And on earth peace, goodwill toward men!"*

15 So it was, when the angels had gone away from them into heaven, that the shepherds said to one another, "Let us now go to Bethlehem and see this thing that has come to pass, which the Lord has made known to us." 16 And they came with haste and found Mary and Joseph, and the Babe lying in a manger.

Matthew 2:1-12, NKJV

1 Now after Jesus was born in Bethlehem of Judea in the days of Herod the king, behold, wise men from the East came to Jerusalem, 2 saying, "Where is He who has been born King of the Jews? For we have seen His star in the East and have come to worship Him."

3 When Herod the king heard this, he was troubled, and all Jerusalem with him. 4 And when he had gathered all the chief priests and scribes of the people together, he inquired of them where the Christ was to be born. 5 So they said to him "In Bethlehem of Judea, for thus it is written by the prophet:

6 'But you, Bethlehem, in the land of Judah, Are not the least among the rulers of Judah; For out of you shall come a Ruler Who will shepherd My people Israel.'"

7 Then Herod, when he had secretly called the wise men, determined from them what time the star appeared. 8 And he sent them to Bethlehem and said, "Go and search carefully for the young Child, and when you have found Him, bring back word to me, that I may come and worship Him also."

> *⁹ When they heard the king, they departed; and behold, the star which they had seen in the East went before them, till it came and stood over where the young Child was. ¹⁰ When they saw the star, they rejoiced with exceedingly great joy. ¹¹ And when they had come into the house, they saw the young Child with Mary His mother, and fell down and worshiped Him. And when they had opened their treasures, they presented gifts to Him: gold, frankincense, and myrrh. ¹² Then, being divinely warned in a dream that they should not return to Herod, they departed for their own country another way.*

Here we have the full arc of the human experience, represented by the poor shepherds and the rich wise men. The haves and the have-nots. The powerful and the powerless. Can you see what this is telling us? Can you begin to tap into your own Mary Mind and be open to this story's very personal message?

The parable is asking us to see *ourselves* in these archetypes. All of us are somewhere between a shepherd and a wise man. We may have a little, we may have a lot, or we may be living in the middle, but we *are* in this story and it *is* speaking to us.

If you are like the shepherds, it may look like you have less in this world. Unlike the wise men who brought gold, frankincense and myrrh, there is no mention in the story of any gifts from the shepherds. They traveled with few possessions and arrived at the manger with little more than their empty hands. But don't be fooled, when the shepherds arrived they did bring a gift. It was really the only thing you can bring on a spiritual quest. Your Self.

The Mary Mind

If you are more like the wise men, then you travel with the gold, frankincense and myrrh of this world. There has been much written about the meaning of these three gifts, but what we have come to see is that when the wise men finally found Jesus and offered up their treasures to him, they were giving up their *attachments to what they thought was of value in their world.* The giving up of these gifts symbolizes their letting go of a mind that valued the valueless, worshiped the worthless and had forgotten Peace and Love. It is the literal demonstration of giving the mind to Christ Consciousness. It is the moment of their enlightenment. It is their shift from The Joseph Mind to The Mary Mind.

The journeys of the shepherds and the wise men were very different. In Luke it says that the shepherds arrived soon after the birth of Jesus and found him lying in the manger. The wise men however didn't find Jesus until much later. Contrary to the popular story told in churches, acted out in "living nativities," and set up in crèches around the world, the Bible does not say the wise men found Jesus in the manger. In Matthew 2:1-12, we're told that they found him in a house with his mother. Historians say that the wise men from the East may have been on their journey for over two years before they found Jesus.

The moral of this parable is that the weight of the baggage we carry determines the length of our journey. When we travel with less on our backs, like the shepherds, our path to Christ Consciousness can take less time. But when we saddle our camels with heavy loads like the wise men, the nights are long and can seem endless.

The Mary Mind

Enlightenment comes, but it's further down the road. In the end, all paths will eventually lead to Peace and Love, but when we carry less in this world the obstacles to enlightenment are fewer and time collapses. We arrive a little sooner at the manger.

This doesn't mean to give up your job or the things you have in this world. It's just telling you to look at your *attachment* to them and ask yourself if they have caused you to lose sight of the Truth that *your life's purpose is to move toward the Awakening of Peace and the Enlightenment of Love.* It may take one moment or a thousand lifetimes, if you believe in that, to burn through all the attachments. But like the wise men, you will come to understand that the journey ends with empty hands and an open mind. You arrive with only Peace and Love.

We are all on a spiritual journey. At any point you can drop your baggage and set aside the things that no longer serve you. Most of us don't unpack all at once. We drop some bags here and some bags there, but as we continue to wander in the night, each pound of gold, frankincense and myrrh we leave behind lessens our burden and quickens our final destination.

Remember, when we talk about baggage we're not talking about possessions − we're talking about our *mental and emotional attachments*. In the Bible, these attachments are expressed through the seven deadly sins of envy, gluttony, greed, lust, pride, sloth, and wrath. They are the cause of every single problem in our world. Every. Single. Problem.

Let's Review

We hope you've been open enough, even just a little, to take in and consider what we've said so far. Let's recap.

1. Mary is our role model. When she came face-to-face with a spiritual Truth that defied what she knew as possible, she set aside the *facts* and was open to the *Truth.* She opened her mind to the mystical Christ Consciousness.

2. Joseph is the rational, ego, human mind that most of us work with on a daily basis.

3. The birth of Jesus can be seen as the birth of Christ Consciousness.

4. You are on a spiritual journey whether you realize it or not.

5. The amount of baggage you carry will determine the length of your journey.

6. Your baggage is nothing more than mental and emotional attachments.

7. The story of Jesus is the story of a man who let go of his baggage and is showing us how to let go of ours.

The New Thought Meets the Old

This is the conversation we must all have with ourselves when our old beliefs just don't work for us any longer.

We've looked at the birth of Jesus and some ideas about what that story means. Now, let's move on to what we know, or don't know, about the early years of Jesus' life.

Oddly, the gospels don't have much to say about the childhood of Jesus. After the story of his birth, the next time Jesus shows up is as a young boy around the age of 12. In Luke 2:41-52, we are told that Joseph, Mary, Jesus and others traveled to Jerusalem for Passover. On their trip back home to Nazareth, Joseph and Mary realize that Jesus is not with them and that he must have been left behind in Jerusalem. They return to the city and when they find him he is in a temple having deep conversations with the teachers, or the rabbis and elders.

> Luke 2: 41-52, NKJV
>
> *[41] His parents went to Jerusalem every year at the Feast of the Passover. [42] And when He was twelve years old, they went up to Jerusalem according to the custom of the feast. [43] When they had finished the days, as they returned, the Boy Jesus lingered behind in Jerusalem. And Joseph and His mother did not know it; [44] but supposing Him to have been in the company, they went a day's journey, and sought Him among their relatives and acquaintances. [45] So when they did not find Him, they returned to Jerusalem, seeking Him. [46] Now so it was that after three days they found Him in the*

> *temple, sitting in the midst of the teachers, both listening to them and asking them questions.*
>
> *⁴⁷ And all who heard Him were astonished at his understanding and answers.*

This "young Jesus in the temple" story is important to our new way of looking at the parables in the Bible and understanding what they are telling us about ourselves. Don't forget that point – these stories about Jesus are a spiritual map to our own awakening.

Let's dive into two details that are key to unlocking this parable's deeper meaning. First, we learn that Jesus is missing, and second we learn that Joseph and Mary find him back in Jerusalem sitting with teachers who were, *"astonished at His understanding and answers."*

Looking at the first detail, Jesus not being with his family on their trip back to Nazareth, it might seem a little negligent of his parents, right? They arrive in Jerusalem for Passover with their son but then lose track of him when they head back home. How could they do that? Especially since Jesus was clearly a very special boy, being born to a virgin and all. You'd think that Mary and Joseph would be "helicopter parents" and keep a close eye on their son, certainly not leaving him behind on the family trip.

When you look at this detail and wonder, *"How* could Jesus have been left behind?" you stir up The Joseph Mind. Its linear thinking is rigid and looks for the so called "facts" in the story instead of looking for the Truth of the parable. But, if you take a breath and give The Mary Mind an opportunity to come forward, the question of *how* slips away and you can ask yourself *why* Jesus separated from his family.

The answer to *why* has to do with Jesus' spiritual evolution. Jesus, the Christ Consciousness, represents a new thought or understanding about God. This new concept has nothing to do with an entity sitting on some cloud creating famine and floods, passing judgment, demanding atonement, ruling dietary laws and deciding who wins or loses a war. That was the Old Testament's story of God. Jesus is here with a new message that *the kingdom of God is within.* The Christ Consciousness understands that God is Love, and that the kingdom of Love is a *state of mind* which is expressed, or witnessed, in how we think, live, practice and cultivate Peace in our lives.

This new and personal concept of God was very different from the traditional teachings of the time. So for Jesus to move toward the full embrace of his awakening, he had to separate himself from the old ideas, beliefs and thought patterns which are represented in this parable by his home in Nazareth and his family. Like anyone who starts down a new path or sees an unorthodox way of doing something, Jesus had to distance himself from the old ways. That's what happens in this story. Jesus separating from his family shows us that for the Christ Consciousness to be born and grow in him, he had to leave the past behind and say goodbye to what was familiar.

The second detail we're looking at in this parable is when Jesus is found in the temple talking with the teachers. This is a profound moment. It is the moment of conversion from the old, "God is out there," way of thinking represented by the traditional teachers in the temple, to the birth of the new thought of Christ Consciousness represented by Jesus, who knows that God is Love and that Love is not "out there." Love is as close as the next thought.

The Mary Mind

Applying this to our own lives, we can see that this is the conversation we must all have with ourselves when our old beliefs just don't work for us any longer. The meeting in the temple represents the life-altering revolution that happens to us the moment we understand that the temple is within. This is when our understanding about God is "born again," and we begin to make the choice and practice of Peace an active part of our daily thinking and living. This is the transformation of The Joseph Mind into The Mary Mind.

The Missing Years

Spiritual development is not a strict curriculum.

After the story of Jesus as a young boy in the temple, the Bible doesn't mention him again until he is about 30 years old. We don't get to read about his developmental years, his schooling or how he learned the spiritual Truths that formed his teachings as an adult. He is basically missing in action until he appears at the river Jordan ready to be baptized by his cousin, John the Baptist.

Does it strike you as strange that the years in which Jesus grew from a young boy into a spiritual mystic are not in the gospels? We found that to be a puzzle. Why would the foundational years of the most written about man to ever live be missing from the Bible?

To find an answer, you have to let go of The Joseph Mind that wants to know *what* is missing. The Joseph Mind wants to know the details. Where did he go? What did he do? Who did he study with?

When you look with The Joseph Mind for "what" is missing, you're looking for proof – you want solid information about exactly what happened. It's the human way, the ego doing its job. But when you release that mind and begin to work with The Mary Mind, you become open and receptive to a different kind of thinking. You let go of the, "*what* is missing," and you ask, "*why* is it missing?" With The Mary Mind you start to read between the lines.

The Mary Mind gives us an answer to "why" which is kind and encouraging. It can be compared to a loving parent watching a child grow and develop strengths and talents on their own. The parent offers sensible guidance, but doesn't micro-manage the child into becoming what the parent wants the child to be. The child is free to explore, try things and eventually become the realized adult that is the result of the experiences the child had as he or she grew up and matured.

The answer The Mary Mind gives us is that the Bible does not include the developmental or "missing years" of Jesus because that would micro-manage *our* experiences. It would lead people and religious institutions to declare that the only way to "salvation" is to do it the way Jesus did it. This would invalidate the millions of spiritual paths people have traveled as they followed their own light in the sky.

Spiritual development is not a strict curriculum. There is no single way to Christ Consciousness. Enlightenment can come to anyone, regardless of who they are, where they come from or what experiences they have had. That's the whole message of the shepherds and the wise men. Our baggage may look different and our journeys may take us down different roads, but everyone's final destination is Peace and Love.

Hard Times Are Bound to Come

*Whether we are paying attention to it or not,
every single one of us is currently on a spiritual path.*

Jesus really steps into his life of Peace and Love at about the age of 30, after he's baptized in the river Jordan.

Matthew 3:13-17, NKJV

[13] Then Jesus came from Galilee to John at the Jordan to be baptized by him. [14] And John tried to prevent Him, saying, "I need to be baptized by You, and are You coming to me?"

[15] But Jesus answered and said to him, "Permit it to be so now, for thus it is fitting for us to fulfill all righteousness." Then he allowed Him.

[16] When He had been baptized, Jesus came up immediately from the water; and behold, the heavens were opened to Him, and He saw the Spirit of God descending like a dove and alighting upon Him. [17] And suddenly a voice came from heaven, saying, "This is My beloved Son, in whom I am well pleased."

Jesus' baptism is his spiritual declaration. Being laid down in water and lifted back up is symbolic of starting a new life. The old one is washed away and there's a feeling of being closer to God, or Love.

Have you been baptized? Or if not baptized, how about a ceremony or tradition that marked your commitment to a spiritual practice, belief or life? Getting baptized or having a spiritual ceremony of some kind is like drawing a line in the sand and saying, "From this point on, I'm going to live my life by certain principles and let go of habits, thinking patterns and life choices that are disaffirming to those principles."

But, do our challenges in life stop at that point? Does our spiritual commitment instantly turn our lives into rainbows and kittens? Does a baptism release us from the insatiable hunger of our ego, the fragility of our body or the power-driven wars in our lives and on the battlefields? You know the answer to that, right?

Well, the same is true for Jesus. After his baptism, Jesus faced his own demons and was taken into the wilderness to be confronted by the devil.

> Luke 4:1-13, NKJV
>
> *Then Jesus, being filled with the Holy Spirit, returned from the Jordan and was led by the Spirit into the wilderness, [2] being tempted for forty days by the devil. And in those days He ate nothing, and afterward, when they had ended, He was hungry.*
>
> *[3] And the devil said to Him, "If You are the Son of God, command this stone to become bread." [4] But Jesus answered him, saying, "It is written, 'Man shall not live by bread alone, but by every word of God.'"*
>
> *[5] Then the devil, taking Him up on a high mountain, showed Him all the kingdoms of the world in a moment of time. [6] And the devil said to Him, "All this authority I will give You, and their glory; for this has been delivered to me, and I give it to whomever I wish. [7] Therefore, if You will worship before me, all will be Yours."*

⁸ And Jesus answered and said to him, "Get behind Me, Satan! For it is written, 'You shall worship the LORD your God, and Him only you shall serve.' "

⁹ Then he brought Him to Jerusalem, set Him on the pinnacle of the temple, and said to Him, "If You are the Son of God, throw Yourself down from here. ¹⁰ For it is written: 'He shall give His angels charge over you, To keep you,' ¹¹ and, 'In their hands they shall bear you up, Lest you dash your foot against a stone.'" ¹² And Jesus answered and said to him, "It has been said, 'You shall not tempt the LORD your God.'"

¹³ Now when the devil had ended every temptation, he departed from Him until an opportune time.

Let's look at this story of wilderness and temptation so it's relevant to us. When we remember that the entire story of Jesus, from his birth to his death, is our own personal guide to enlightenment, we can see these temptations by "the devil" with a different mindset.

Jesus' faith was tested in the wilderness even after his full embrace of a spiritual life. This is true for any spiritual seeker. Haven't you experienced, "the dark night of the soul," where you felt lost and alone in the world, out in the wilderness, confronted with circumstances that just seem to be more than you can bear?

When we are on a spiritual path, whatever that path may be, hard times are bound to come – death, job loss, family dysfunction, economic fear. The list goes on and on, but in this Bible story the hard times, or temptations, are whittled down to just three.

The Mary Mind

1. Turning stones into bread: We see hunger, which symbolizes all our outward needs, addictions and materialist clinging.
2. Worshiping the devil: We see the crippling temptation of power, or the ego.
3. Throwing himself off a high pinnacle: We see the fear of death.

That pretty much sums up our lives doesn't it? Life's big trials, tests and temptations are our devils for sure, but don't forget the smaller distractions and ongoing chatter that also fight for our attention. Together, these are the deafening voices that tell us to feed our materialistic hunger instead of dropping our baggage; seek outward power instead of inward knowledge; and tend to our body's needs instead of our spiritual needs. These are the false idols we have put before God, or Love. No wonder our lives can seem void of real meaning and we find it almost impossible to, "be still and know that I am God."

The entire world is a fast-food smorgasbord for our five senses – a buffet set up and designed to serve us with chaos. This world causes us to forget we have The Mary Mind and delays our spiritual journey by keeping us constantly distracted, busy, worried, confused and stuck in The Joseph Mind.

But the journey *is* happening, and it's happening right now. Whether we are paying attention to it or not, every one of us is on a spiritual path. The scenery may look different, we may see poverty or wealth, illness or health, but in the end, all journeys lead to Christ Consciousness, Enlightenment, Heaven, Love or whatever you want to call it. Jesus is showing us the destination and Mary is showing us the mind that makes the trip.

The Apostles

*Their differences didn't separate them,
because their common direction joined them.*

So Jesus had a posse.

1. Andrew
2. Bartholomew
3. James
4. James
5. John
6. Judas
7. Matthew
8. Philip
9. Simon
10. Simon/Peter
11. Thaddaeus
12. Thomas

These are the 12 guys that the Bible says were Jesus' inner circle and who he pretty much hand-picked. Being chosen by a messiah surely means that these guys were special. They got to witness miracles like bodily healing, multiplying bread and fish, raising the dead and of course, Jesus' resurrection. In fact, after his resurrection, Jesus thought so much of these disciples that he sent them out into the world (well, not Judas) to spread his teaching (Matthew 28:16-20).

The apostles were clearly the A-team. To most of us, they seem to be the untouchables, so close to Jesus that we couldn't have much in common with them. And don't forget that most of them were made saints. That really puts them in a league of their own.

Stories about the apostles vary in the Bible and it is not our place to debate any of those writings. We are just here to make a little room for interpreting some of the stories in ways you may not have considered.

First, let's look at the lives of the apostles before they were "the" apostles. They had jobs or vocations, several working in family businesses or trades, and overall were probably average citizens in their communities. In other words, they were like most of us – we get up, go to work, come home, grab some dinner, spend some time with friends and family and then head off to bed. Not exactly apostle material.

Next, let's think about their decision to become followers of Jesus. It's not like they applied for the job of "apostle" or anything. They simply felt a calling or had an experience that ignited their dedication to a spiritual ideal or path. Each of them basically dropped what they were doing to follow a teacher named Jesus and embark on a new way of life. We could say this was their conversion to The Mary Mind, the shift where they began to be aware of their *choice* for a Mind of Peace instead of their *choice* for a mind without Peace, or The Joseph Mind.

This awareness of the choice is the Christ Consciousness becoming lit, or enlightened, in them, and by example in us. Eventually, there will be no choice to make – Peace will have made itself at home in your Mind and will be as natural as breathing. Every response to every thought you have will be Peaceful. The days for decision making will be over because all the Mind knows is Peace. This is when you are truly *in Love*, or one with God.

The Mary Mind

This sounds pretty heady, so how do we relate to that? For starters, look at your life and find a moment that caused you to pause and question an idea, change an opinion, examine a belief or the way you thought about someone. We've all had these moments, so find one in your life. As minor as it may have seemed at the time, ask yourself if it interrupted the everyday-kind-of-thinking you were used to. Did this moment of "new thought" cause you to change something about your life? If so, this was a conversion moment. And, if this conversion moment was triggered by a spiritual insight, understanding or thought, then this could be called a rebirth, and it's a direct connection to The Mary Mind. Just like the disciples who had their conversion moments and were called to follow Jesus, this new direction or call in our life makes *us* apostles.

Of course the lives we lead today are very different than those of the Biblical apostles. We usually don't quit our jobs, give up everything we own and roam town to town with our guru. But that doesn't disqualify us from being an apostle. On the spiritual journey, no two lives walk the same path. The disciples themselves had different and unique experiences from each other, but that didn't mean one could be an apostle and another not. Their differences didn't separate them, because their common purpose joined them.

The apostles were nothing but students. When they left their old lives they knew little about Jesus or his teaching. But they felt a calling and began to listen to this teacher who was ripping the curtain down from the church altar that separated the people from God. Jesus was telling them that God was not in a building or at a sacred site; *God was Love,* and it was inside of them.

That's how we can relate to the 12 apostles. Like them, we can have a spiritual experience that slowly, or instantly, changes the direction of our lives. Then, we go out and be the expression of Peace and Love, which is all that Jesus asked his disciples to do.

It's a Miracle!

The miracles of Jesus are a fundamental element in the gospels. For millions of Christians around the world, miracles are the building blocks of their faith in Jesus as their Savior.

We don't want to take away the importance of Jesus' miracles in the Bible. After all, being able to walk on water is a pretty big deal. We're not arguing that point, but let's go deeper than just general interpretations of the miracles. Remember, we're looking at the miracles as parables with a moral. And it's these morals, which are spiritual Truths, that need to be unlocked in your mind before they can be opened in your heart.

Let's organize the miracles into four basic categories, and then we'll look at one story from each group.

1. Raising the dead
2. Healing
3. Abundance
4. Control of nature

Of course, we're not going to forget about the resurrection, but we'll talk about that later. And, there's one more miracle we want to include that doesn't really fall into any of these categories – the turning of water into wine. Let's start there, since it is the first miracle that Jesus performs and an important prelude to the other miracles. The water into wine story shows us how we get to the point of "enough is enough," and prepares us for the transformational cleanse of our minds and our lives.

The Miracle of Turning Water into Wine

Our lives are the inferior wine that has intoxicated us into thinking we are fulfilled.

John 2:1-10, NKJV

On the third day there was a wedding in Cana of Galilee, and the mother of Jesus was there. ²Now both Jesus and His disciples were invited to the wedding. ³And when they ran out of wine, the mother of Jesus said to Him, "They have no wine." ⁴Jesus said to her, "Woman, what does your concern have to do with Me? My hour has not yet come."

⁵His mother said to the servants, "Whatever He says to you, do it." ⁶Now there were set there six waterpots of stone, according to the manner of purification of the Jews, containing twenty or thirty gallons apiece. ⁷Jesus said to them, "Fill the waterpots with water." And they filled them up to the brim. ⁸And He said to them, "Draw some out now, and take it to the master of the feast." And they took it. ⁹When the master of the feast had tasted the water that was made wine, and did not know where it came from (but the servants who had drawn the water knew), the master of the feast called the bridegroom. ¹⁰And he said to him, "Every man at the beginning sets out the good wine, and when the guests have well drunk, then the inferior. You have kept the good wine until now!"

The Mary Mind

This is Jesus' first miracle. He turns water into wine. That's it. Compared to raising the dead, this miracle kind of feels like a parlor trick. On a first reading maybe so, but you know what we're going to do, don't you? That's right! We're going to break it down and find a new way to see what this parable is telling us. As straightforward as the story may sound, turning water into wine, it in fact goes right to the heart of *The Mary Mind*.

The first thing we're going to think about is the event that is taking place in this story – a wedding. Now to most of us, a wedding is a pretty clear thing – two people hitching their wagons to each other. But as a *spiritual idea*, a wedding is the joining of two energies – the giving with the receiving, the yin with the yang, the heart with the mind, man with the Christ Consciousness. It is the transfiguration of the two into one.

Next, let's dig into the meaning of the wine. We usually think of wine as a fragrant red or dry white that adds a nice touch to a meal, conversation or even a romantic evening. But in churches and religious communities, wine represents the actual blood of Christ, and when it's taken in communion, it is symbolically joining you with Jesus, or the Christ Consciousness.

Take a minute to collect your thoughts and think about the story so far:

1. We have a wedding, which is the *idea* of joining together man and Christ Consciousness.
2. The wedding has run out of wine, which is the *idea* of man not being able to be joined or filled with the Christ Consciousness.

Now that we've looked at the meaning of the wedding and the wine, let's move on to the conversation between Jesus and his mother. Mary says to Jesus, *"They have no more wine,"* to which Jesus responds, *"Woman, what does your concern have to do with Me? My hour has not yet come."*

Does this feel a little dismissive and out of character for a man who is filled with the Holy Spirit? It certainly might, until we look at it from a different perspective.

First off, when Jesus refers to his mother as, "Woman," he is not being disrespectful. That term is simply a matter of translation and pretty much means the same thing as "Ma'am," which is a term of respectful or polite address used for a woman. So don't get hung up on that word.

Next, when Mary turns to Jesus and says, *"They have no more wine,"* it may seem like she's asking him to perform a miracle by restocking the bar. But that's not what is happening here. Mary knows the problem *and* the solution, and it has nothing to do with the wine.

Mary is showing *us* what to do when our wine, *or our communion with the Christ Consciousness*, is gone. We may feel like our lives have fallen apart or become meaningless and without direction. But it's at this point, when we are in our darkest place, that Mary shines and becomes our example, leading us toward the solution.

Mary understands that at life's low moments, the Christ Consciousness needs to be *spiritually summoned*. So when she goes to Jesus, she is not asking him to provide more booze; she is in fact, moving into prayer. She is calling up the Christ Consciousness, connecting with that Mind that is inside, but beyond, herself. This is The Mary Mind connecting to Truth, knowing it will supply what is needed

The Mary Mind

– a Mind that is open to purification, Peace and the continual communion of man with Love, or God.

With this interpretation, let's now consider what Jesus means when he says that he is not concerned with the lack of wine and that his hour has not yet come. First, we need to jump ahead just a bit and look at what the "master of the feast," or *maitre d'*, says about the good wine and the inferior wine. In layman's terms, he is saying that contrary to the usual practice of getting the guests drunk on the good wine first so they won't notice when the cheap stuff is brought out, at this wedding the inferior wine has been served first. Now why would that be? To get the answer, we have to dig beneath the surface meaning of the words and look for the moral of this parable.

The guests have gotten drunk on the inferior wine, and now the wine jugs are empty. In other words, the wine, which represents the blood of Christ or *the sustenance of life that is the Christ Consciousness*, has run out and is gone from everyone at the wedding. It's at this point that Mary speaks to Jesus and in turn Jesus speaks to *us*. He tells us that the lack of the *inferior* wine is not his concern and that his hour has not come. Use your Mary Mind here to open up the parable and see the symbolism of what is unfolding.

What Jesus is talking about has nothing to do with wine. He is talking about our spiritual lives and pointing out in metaphoric language that we are living without true life energy, without being open to enlightenment, without the sustenance of the *best* wine or the Christ Consciousness. We have become so intoxicated on inferior wine that we now believe an inferior life is acceptable. But at some point the drunk wears off.

When this happens, we might experience our darkest hour. It may manifest as a "midlife crisis," where we divorce, have an affair, pick up alcohol, drugs or other addictions, move, buy a car, have a child, travel, overspend, ruin family relationships, quit a job or a million other things. But this crisis doesn't just prey on midlife. It can show up in our teens or early adulthood, or haunt us later in life when age and experience have left us empty or fearful of death.

Whenever it happens, this becomes our breaking point. This is where the cheap wine runs out and we feel alone, confused, desperate, depressed. The wedding is over.

When we hit this bottom, whether it comes abruptly or as a slow slide down the mountain, it can be devastating. But this moment can also be our rebirth, and the rebirth is what Jesus is talking about when he says he is not concerned with the lack of the inferior wine.

Why would Jesus want to refill your glass with the same inferior wine that has left you drunk, hungover and still so thirsty? Like Mary, Jesus sees the problem and the solution and he's not interested in providing more bathtub gin to the party. He is not going to feed the blind addictions that have kept the guests homeless in their own homes.

Jesus continues his message to us when he says, *"My hour has not yet come."* This is the perfect follow-up to his lack of concern about the inferior wine. He's telling us that the awareness of Christ Consciousness has not yet come *for the guests* at the wedding. They have been fooled by the cheap wine and are unaware that the best wine is still uncorked.

The Mary Mind

Their hour for opening to the Christ Consciousness has not come because they are in the blackout of The Joseph Mind.

The story moves forward with Mary again giving us a message when she tells the servants, *"Whatever He says to you, do it."* These are more than just words – this is another prayer from Mary affirming the Truth. She is activating our Mary Mind – telling us to listen to the inner voice and *whatever it says to you, do it.* You might call that voice God, Jesus, Holy Spirit, Inner Child, Higher Self or whatever, but to connect with it you have to have the willingness to go into your "altered state" where that voice can be heard.

That voice may show up in prayer, or as intuition. Or, you may run across it in a book or hear it shared in conversation. Wherever you receive the message, if you're open and have even the smallest amount of willingness, The Mary Mind is awakened and your spiritual detox can begin. This is why Jesus now asks for the purification pots to be filled – he's initiating the cleanse that will flush out the inferior wine that has left its sludge in our spiritual veins. It may take years or it may happen in one mystical miraculous moment, but eventually, the toxic mind is baptized and the old self washes away. This is where the water turns to fine wine.

In the final part of this miracle parable, the "master of the feast" is wrapping it up, giving us the moral of the story. He's saying that when we get blind drunk on the world, we become unconscious instead of Christ-conscious. Resentment, envy, pride or any of the other deadly sins overtake us and we forget the Truth and real purpose of our lives – to nurture spiritual growth in ourselves and others by remembering to make the choice for the Mind of Peace in everything we do.

The Miracle of Raising Lazarus From the Dead

This is where Jesus shows human emotion and spiritual devotion.

One of the most famous miracles in the gospels is the story of Jesus raising Lazarus from the dead. Surely, if there was a ranking of miracles, this one would be a headliner. We're not going to try and debunk any of the miracles and certainly not the Lazarus story. We are just trying to make this miracle and the life of Jesus more relatable.

Jesus was a man who became a Master, as he is called many times in the Bible. But we see that as a term of respect for a teacher or a mentor, not a reference to a ruler, king or governing lord. That's what got Jesus into trouble with the religious leaders and political officials of his time. They saw him as a threat to their power because people were listening to him and following wherever he went. We're not making the same mistake – we don't see Jesus as a deity, we see him as a spiritual guide.

This miracle is pretty much a solid bedrock of Christian teaching. It's usually taken literally and used to drive home the point of the absolute power and divinity of Jesus. But like every other miracle in the gospels it can be understood differently than the usual Sunday School lesson many of us knew as children. It is without a doubt about resurrection, but it is not about Lazarus. It is about *our* resurrection from the Lazarus sleep.

The Mary Mind

This story gets our attention by dramatically illustrating the situation most of us are in. We are the sleeping dead, unwilling to awaken, unaware of enlightenment and closed to The Mary Mind. When we read this story with our Joseph Mind, it looks like a story about bringing a dead man back to life. As always, The Joseph Mind can only see things as they appear to be. It tells us to look at the *facts* of this story but to ignore the *Truth* of this story.

Sometimes there is a great difference between facts and Truth. Facts are The Joseph Mind. Truth is The Mary Mind. And as they say, the Truth will set you free.

Now, let's break this story down into three parts.

Part One, John 11:1-4, NKJV: The situation is set up. We're introduced to the main characters, Mary, Martha, Lazarus and Jesus, and we're told what the problem is: Lazarus is very sick.

> *"Now a certain man was sick, Lazarus of Bethany, the town of Mary and her sister Martha. ² It was that Mary who anointed the Lord with fragrant oil and wiped His feet with her hair, whose brother Lazarus was sick. ³ Therefore the sisters sent to Him, saying, "Lord, behold, he whom You love is sick." ⁴ When Jesus heard that, He said, "This sickness is not unto death, but for the glory of God, that the Son of God be glorified through it."*

If you really grasped what this section is saying, you would understand the whole message of the Lazarus miracle. There are some structural details that are informative narrative, like who Mary and Martha are and their relationship to Lazarus, but we find the jewel of this passage in the dialog.

The Mary Mind

"Lord, behold, he whom You love is sick" is the message that Mary and Martha send to Jesus. At first, it seems like an appropriate note to send, but when you read it again, it seems rather open-ended. The sisters don't specifically say, "Lazarus is sick," they just say, *"he whom You love is sick."* This is a key point. True to a parable's format where one character or an idea can represent a larger, more universal concept, the character of Lazarus represents not just one man who appears to be sick, but everyone who has fallen into the Lazarus sleep of unawareness.

As the story moves along, we see how Jesus responds to the sister's plea for help. The passage reads:

> *5 When he heard that Lazarus was sick, he said, "This sickness is not unto death, but for the glory of God, that the Son of God may be glorified through it."*

Here is one of those great chasms between the facts and the Truth. We think the problem is the fact that Lazarus is sick and close to death. Jesus however, ignores the *fact* that his friend is sick and lays out the *Truth*. He knows that the sickness that infects Lazarus, and all mankind, does not lead to death because it is not the body that needs healing. The sickness that has us in its grip is in our mind, and the cure is to awaken our Mary Mind to the *choice* for thoughts of Peace, and leave our Joseph Mind in its grave of unconsciousness.

Part Two, John 11:5-16: In this section, the disciples are brought into the story as a sort of chorus of our own fear and doubting thoughts. They don't understand anything that Jesus is telling them in his parabolic style. Don't forget, the disciples are not enlightened Masters, they are just students following and learning from their teacher.

5 Now Jesus loved Martha and her sister and Lazarus. 6 So, when He heard that he was sick, He stayed two more days in the place where He was. 7 Then after this He said to the disciples, "Let us go to Judea again." 8 The disciples said to Him, "Rabbi, lately the Jews sought to stone You, and are You going there again?" 9 Jesus answered, "Are there not twelve hours in the day? If anyone walks in the day, he does not stumble, because he sees the light of this world. 10 But if one walks in the night, he stumbles, because the light is not in him." 11 These things He said, and after that He said to them, "Our friend Lazarus sleeps, but I go that I may wake him up."

12 Then His disciples said, "Lord, if he sleeps he will get well." 13 However, Jesus spoke of his death, but they thought that He was speaking about taking rest in sleep. 14 Then Jesus said to them plainly, "Lazarus is dead. 15 And I am glad for your sakes that I was not there, that you may believe. Nevertheless let us go to him." 16 Then Thomas, who is called the Twin, said to his fellow disciples, "Let us also go, that we may die with Him."

We said earlier that the apostles represent us, and here we see them making excuses and finding reasons for Jesus not to go see Lazarus. The disciples seem to be trying to protect Jesus from being stoned, but in fact, they are fearful for their own safety, scared of being stoned themselves. This is why Thomas, after getting a little tongue-lashing from Jesus, eventually resigns himself to his fate and tells the other apostles, *"Let us also go, that we may die with Him."*

In the story, the disciples' fear of joining with Jesus and awakening Lazarus represents *our* own fear of connecting with Christ Consciousness and awakening. On some level, we realize that waking up from our Lazarus sleep means the end of life as we know it, and that scares us. This is our Joseph Mind in action recoiling from the Light and shutting down our link to Christ Consciousness. In a confused and fearful state of mind, we believe as the apostles did, that being brought back to life will kill us. And in a metaphoric way, that's right – *awakening is a transformational death.*

This transformation can be experienced as anything from mildly uncomfortable to absolutely terrifying. Jesus addresses this rocky road when he talks about walking in the day versus the night. He tells us that when we walk in the Light of Christ Consciousness the stones along the way are less likely to trip us up. But when we wander around in the darkness the rocks on the road cause us to stumble and fall. There will always be rough roads, but there will also always be Light to walk with you.

Part Three, John 11:17-44: In this section we are at the scene where the real action takes place. Jesus is taken to the cave where Lazarus is buried and calls for him to rise.

> [17] *So when Jesus came, He found that he had already been in the tomb four days.* [18] *Now Bethany was near Jerusalem, about two miles away.* [19] *And many of the Jews had joined the women around Martha and Mary, to comfort them concerning their brother.* [20] *Now Martha, as soon as she heard that Jesus was coming, went and met Him, but Mary was sitting in the house.* [21] *Now Martha said to Jesus, "Lord, if You had been here, my brother would not have died.* [22] *But even now I know that whatever You ask of God, God will give You."*

²³ Jesus said to her, "Your brother will rise again." ²⁴ Martha said to Him, "I know that he will rise again in the resurrection at the last day." ²⁵ Jesus said to her, "I am the resurrection and the life. He who believes in Me, though he may die, he shall live. ²⁶ And whoever lives and believes in Me shall never die. Do you believe this?" ²⁷ She said to Him, "Yes, Lord, I believe that You are the Christ, the Son of God, who is to come into the world."

²⁸ And when she had said these things, she went her way and secretly called Mary her sister, saying, "The Teacher has come and is calling for you." ²⁹ As soon as she heard that, she arose quickly and came to Him. ³⁰ Now Jesus had not yet come into the town, but was in the place where Martha met Him. ³¹ Then the Jews who were with her in the house, and comforting her, when they saw that Mary rose up quickly and went out, followed her, saying, "She is going to the tomb to weep there." ³² Then, when Mary came where Jesus was, and saw Him, she fell down at His feet, saying to Him, "Lord, if You had been here, my brother would not have died." ³³ Therefore, when Jesus saw her weeping, and the Jews who came with her weeping, He groaned in the spirit and was troubled. ³⁴ And He said, "Where have you laid him?" They said to Him, "Lord, come and see." ³⁵ Jesus wept. ³⁶ Then the Jews said, "See how He loved him!" ³⁷ And some of them said, "Could not this Man, who opened the eyes of the blind, also have kept this man from dying?"

³⁸ Then Jesus, again groaning in Himself, came to the tomb. It was a cave, and a stone lay against it. ³⁹ Jesus said, "Take away the stone." Martha, the

The Mary Mind

> *sister of him who was dead, said to Him, "Lord, by this time there is a stench, for he has been dead four days." ⁴⁰ Jesus said to her, "Did I not say to you that if you would believe you would see the glory of God?" ⁴¹ Then they took away the stone from the place where the dead man was lying. And Jesus lifted up His eyes and said, "Father, I thank You that You have heard Me. ⁴² And I know that You always hear Me, but because of the people who are standing by I said this, that they may believe that You sent Me." ⁴³ Now when He had said these things, He cried with a loud voice, "Lazarus, come forth!" ⁴⁴ And he who had died came out bound hand and foot with graveclothes, and his face was wrapped with a cloth. Jesus said to them, "Loose him, and let him go."*

There is so much information in this passage, but we want to get to the heart of the matter. This is where Jesus shows his human emotion and spiritual devotion.

First and foremost, this is an intensely moving portrait of Jesus the man and Jesus the Christ Consciousness. In this section, he weeps and groans and comforts family members Mary and Martha, but he also never loses touch with his spiritual center. Regardless of the *fact* of human grief in this story, Jesus does not step out of the pure Light of *Truth*.

Again, this parable is not about Lazarus, it's not about raising a man from the dead and it's not even about Jesus. This is a story about us and the resurrection of *our* minds. The cave that holds the sleeping Lazarus is not a tomb, it's a prison. It's *our* locked-down belief that we are somehow separated from or unconnected to God, or the Love that Jesus taught. In the *story*, Jesus is indeed weeping with the grieving friends and family. But in the *parable*, he's not weeping for the loss of a loved one – he's weeping for the loss of Love altogether. He's weeping for all of *us* who believe God is somewhere, "out there," instead of, "in here," as a part of us. And this breaks his very human heart.

In the final verses, Jesus performs the miracle, an act of pure Love for all who can see. But first, he prays. He expresses gratitude for his own awareness of Love in everything he experiences and he asks that all who witness the miracle also wake up to the awareness of Love.

Then Jesus calls to Lazarus, as he calls to us, to arise and leave the darkness. He beckons all of us to step into the Light and be free of the gravesclothes that have covered our eyes, deafened our ears and deadened our minds to the awareness and enlightenment of the Christ Consciousness and Love.

The Miracle of Healing the 10 Lepers

We have to commit to a path that will heal us,
not just fix us.

There are quite a few miracle stories in the gospels that involve the healing of one type of ailment or another. A few of the afflictions are blindness, bleeding, disease and the inability to speak or hear. The parable we're going to look at in the healing category is found in Luke and involves the healing of leprosy.

> Luke 17:11-19, NKJV
>
> [11] *Now it happened as He went to Jerusalem that He passed through the midst of Samaria and Galilee.* [12] *Then as He entered a certain village, there met Him ten men who were lepers, who stood afar off.* [13] *And they lifted up their voices and said, "Jesus, Master, have mercy on us!"*
>
> [14] *So when He saw them, He said to them, "Go, show yourselves to the priests." And so it was that as they went, they were cleansed.*
>
> [15] *And one of them, when he saw that he was healed, returned, and with a loud voice glorified God,* [16] *and fell down on his face at His feet, giving Him thanks. And he was a Samaritan.*
>
> [17] *So Jesus answered and said, "Were there not ten cleansed? But where are the nine?* [18] *Were there not any found who returned to give glory to God except this foreigner?"* [19] *And He said to him, "Arise, go your way. Your faith has made you well."*

On the surface, this story seems to be about leprosy and Jesus' supernatural power to cure the disease. Common interpretations of this miracle focus on the ability to heal as validation that Jesus is a special being sent from God.

Of course, we see the story as something quite different and personal. Jesus is our teacher, or as he's called in this parable, "Master," and he's showing us the way to our own healing through the process of purification of the mind, just like in the "turning water to wine" miracle we looked at earlier in this book.

Let's pull this story apart by first thinking about leprosy. At the time of Jesus, leprosy was of course a disease, but it was also seen as a condition of "impurity." The treatment might call for priests to come in and perform a purification process dedicated to God that could involve water, animal sacrifice, prayer and more. In other words, the purification process was to appease a God "out there" in exchange for a cure. When Jesus came along and could heal leprosy on the spot, of course he seemed like a miracle worker and the true Son of God. But let's look beyond the obvious and see this parable through the clarity of The Mary Mind.

We have 10 lepers asking to be healed by Jesus who, as we've said many times, represents *the manifested idea of the Christ Consciousness.* When Jesus is called upon to cure the lepers he doesn't just wave a healing hand and end the story there. No, he tells the lepers, *"Go, show yourselves to the priests."* For their healing to manifest, the lepers had to go through a purification period, which is represented by Jesus sending them to the priests.

Everything in this story is more than it appears to be. The priests are a metaphor for the purification process; leprosy is not a disease of the body, but rather a disease or impurity

The Mary Mind

of the mind; and the lepers represent us, or anyone who has that diseased state of mind instead of a mind that is in a state of Peace. The disease against Peace is what's eating us alive – and this virus has not come from without, it has come from within.

Our leprosy cannot be healed with medicine. No pill will cure, no surgery will fix and no x-ray will find the cause. Our disease goes deeper. The illness is inside *us*, not our bodies. The cure, like Jesus implies, does not come directly from him but from a spiritual purification journey. Like the lepers, we have to walk a path that will heal us, not just fix us.

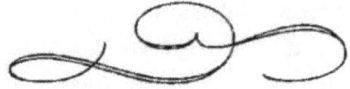

This journey does not have to wait until we hit rock bottom like the lepers. The path to enlightenment is filled with people who began their spiritual practice long before any crash and burn happened in their lives. It doesn't matter whether we are young or old when we start walking a spiritual path because we don't make the journey on our feet, we make it in our minds. Or you could say, we don't make this journey with The Joseph Mind, we make it with The Mary Mind.

It may sound like we keep bashing poor Joseph, but actually The Joseph Mind has served us pretty well. We don't want to make light of its importance, up to a point. It's been a reliable friend, often kept us safe and usually allowed us to function in society. But The Joseph Mind can only go so far with us on the spiritual journey. There comes a time when we have to go further and the trip turns inward. The Joseph Mind can't go there. All it knows is how to look for a God "out there" to heal us, save us, change us, get us a job or send us a lover. We've been like the lepers who were looking for someone outside themselves to cleanse their impurity.

We're not saying that you shouldn't pray for a physical healing. Prayer is a powerful practice and has produced miraculous results. What we're talking about is the idea of prayer and healing as it relates to this parable. Prayer can be many things, and here, Jesus is, in fact, telling the lepers to go and pray when he says, *"Go, show yourselves to the priests."* He is sending them on their prayerful purification journey so they can experience the mindful healing of *Truth,* not just the bodily healing of leprosy.

After the healing happens and only one leper returns to give thanks, the parable says that Jesus asked, *"Were there not ten cleansed? But where are the nine? Were there not any found who returned to give glory to God except this foreigner?"* What did Jesus mean here? Was he throwing a hissy fit and judging the others who had not returned to thank him? Some people might read it that way, but not us. Why would Jesus, who taught only Peace and Love, all the sudden turn into a vengeful (and even a little sarcastic) diva? We don't believe he did, and we don't believe that's what these words mean.

Remember, this is a parable, so the ideas and meanings in the story are bigger than what they appear to be. When Jesus asks the one healed leper about the others, *it's a rhetorical question.* He's not really asking about the other nine. He's asking the one man, *who represents us*, to go inside himself and see that there was really only one problem, one sickness, to be healed. Not 10 or 20 or a billion. Jesus knows that true healing happens when the impurity *leaves your mind*, not your body. So Jesus is asking the one leper to go to inside and look at the source of all illness – his mind.

Our body is the distraction that keeps us from looking at our thinking, and as long as we think the body is what needs attention, we will never find the cure for what ails us.

In this parable, there are 10 different lepers, but it's important to remember that they all have the same disease. Everyone is suffering from the same thing. So *symbolically*, there is only one problem, and *symbolically*, there is only one cure.

This is why only one leper returns to give thanks to Jesus, or the Christ Consciousness. The 10 lepers are a metaphor for the idea of *all of us as one*, who believe we need an endless number of healings, fixes and cures to make our lives "work."

But when we begin our purification journey, like the lepers, we eventually come to the understanding that all of the separate issues, problems, fears and confusion we thought we had, turn out to be just one problem – the belief that something other than Love is the cure.

To get to this Love, you have to practice Peace. To practice Peace, you have to constantly remind yourself to be open to working with The Mary Mind. *This practice is your purification journey.* This is the journey where you remember to be kind – always choosing Peace as you walk toward the Mind of Love, or The Mind of God.

The Miracle of Feeding the 5000

The table is always set, the kitchen is always cooking and there's always a seat at the table waiting for you.

This miracle is short and sweet and feels warm and fuzzy. As a parable, it gently pulls us in by presenting a picture of something most of us can identify with – sitting down at the family table and being nourished by a meal.

John 6:1-14, NKJV

After these things Jesus went over the Sea of Galilee, which is the Sea of Tiberias. ^{2} Then a great multitude followed Him, because they saw His signs which He performed on those who were diseased. ^{3} And Jesus went up on the mountain, and there He sat with His disciples.

^{4} Now the Passover, a feast of the Jews, was near. ^{5} Then Jesus lifted up His eyes, and seeing a great multitude coming toward Him, He said to Philip, "Where shall we buy bread, that these may eat?" ^{6} But this He said to test him, for He Himself knew what He would do.

^{7} Philip answered Him, "Two hundred denarii worth of bread is not sufficient for them, that every one of them may have a little."

^{8} One of His disciples, Andrew, Simon Peter's brother, said to Him, ^{9} "There is a lad here who has five barley loaves and two small fish, but what are they among so many?"

The Mary Mind

¹⁰ Then Jesus said, "Make the people sit down." Now there was much grass in the place. So the men sat down, in number about five thousand. ¹¹And Jesus took the loaves, and when He had given thanks He distributed them to the disciples, and the disciples to those sitting down; and likewise of the fish, as much as they wanted. ¹² So when they were filled, He said to His disciples, "Gather up the fragments that remain, so that nothing is lost." ¹³ Therefore they gathered them up, and filled twelve baskets with the fragments of the five barley loaves which were left over by those who had eaten. ¹⁴ Then those men, when they had seen the sign that Jesus did, said, "This is truly the Prophet who is to come into the world."

This Bible miracle is a favorite in children's Sunday School lessons because they can see themselves in the story. There's no mind-bending walking on water or ghoulish raising the dead. It's simply a picnic with baskets of food. We love this miracle, and after some very heavy stories about Jesus, it feels like a little break. We're invited to sit down and have a bite.

Food is a basic human need and pretty much keeps us alive. So this miracle goes straight to our gut (literally), and makes us feel safe and taken care of because Jesus is in the kitchen and the disciples have called everyone in for dinner. In a way, it's like the famous Norman Rockwell painting of a family having their Thanksgiving meal. We see an abundance of food and all is right with the world.

When we're open to The Mary Mind, this parable becomes more than just a story about filling our plate. Yes, we have an all-you-can-eat buffet of bread and fish, but what this is really talking about is the inexhaustible source of Christ

The Mary Mind

Consciousness. The more you let go of your old ideas about the *facts of life* – having only five loaves and two fish – the more aware you are of the *Truth of life* – your connection to the Christ Consciousness grows in abundance, multiplying itself the more you use it. In other words, it's the opposite of our belief that the more you use something the less you have of it.

As long as we stay at the dinner table, Jesus – *the physical manifestation of the Christ Consciousness* – is serving us a meal that never ends. The more we eat, the more there is to eat. Of course, if we don't let go of The Joseph Mind, then we try to order a different meal, or we have a tendency to think we're full and we ask to be excused from the table. That's when the spiritual food runs out. We've interrupted the endless servings of Love and we're back to the scraps and crumbs. But the Truth about this miracle story is that in reality, the table *is* always set, the kitchen *is* always cooking and there *is* always a seat at the table waiting for us.

The Miracle of Walking on Water and Calming the Sea

Have you ever refused the rescue because it doesn't look like the help you prayed for?

We're combining two miracles into one in this chapter. The miracle story of Jesus walking on water and then calming a tempestuous sea are both in the same parable, so it's natural to tie them together.

With the right perspective, both walking on water and calming the sea are indeed about controlling nature. Not so much the control of nature as in water and wind, but rather nature in the manner of the *nature of things*, or the way in which we believe the world seems to work.

This miracle occurs right after the feeding of the 5000 and is mentioned in Matthew, Mark and John. They are all basically the same story, told in different ways with a few minor differences. We're going to look at the passage from Matthew because it happens to be the version that mentions the Apostle Peter, and we think that's an important piece of the story.

> Matthew 14:22-33, NKJV
>
> *[22] Immediately Jesus made His disciples get into the boat and go before Him to the other side, while He sent the multitudes away. [23] And when He had sent the multitudes away, He went up on the mountain by Himself to pray. Now when evening came, He was alone there. [24] But the boat was now in the middle of the sea, tossed by the waves, for the wind was contrary.*

The Mary Mind

> *^{25} Now in the fourth watch of the night Jesus went to them, walking on the sea. ^{26} And when the disciples saw Him walking on the sea, they were troubled, saying, "It is a ghost!" And they cried out for fear.*
>
> *^{27} But immediately Jesus spoke to them, saying, "Be of good cheer! It is I; do not be afraid." ^{28} And Peter answered Him and said, "Lord, if it is You, command me to come to You on the water."*
>
> *^{29} So He said, "Come." And when Peter had come down out of the boat, he walked on the water to go to Jesus. ^{30} But when he saw that the wind was boisterous, he was afraid; and beginning to sink he cried out, saying, "Lord, save me!"*
>
> *^{31} And immediately Jesus stretched out His hand and caught him, and said to him, "O you of little faith, why did you doubt?" ^{32} And when they got into the boat, the wind ceased. ^{33} Then those who were in the boat came and worshiped Him, saying, "Truly You are the Son of God."*

This story is exhilarating. Not only do we get to see the amazing feat of walking on water (Two times! Or rather, one-and-a-half cause Peter kinda blows his chance), we also get to see Jesus taking control of the elements and shutting down the heavy winds and choppy sea. We really get our money's worth on this one.

Now, let's look at this parable as if it's a play with the apostles in the lead roles. Jesus is still a very important player, but for now let's give him second billing in this production.

As the curtain rises, Jesus has just fed about 5000 people. The apostles witnessed this amazing miracle of abundance and you can pretty much assume they were trying to wrap their heads around what they had seen. Remember, the apostles were *students* of Jesus, not miracle workers themselves. They were still trying to figure things out as they followed this teacher who was schooling them about Peace and Love.

After the 5000 are fed, Jesus instructs the disciples to get in a boat and head out *"to the other side."* He stays behind, sending the multitudes back to their homes and then he retreats up a mountain to pray.

This is an important plot point, because Jesus is now removed from the story for a bit so we can give our full attention to the disciples. The men have rowed out to sea where the wind and waves are, *"contrary,"* which means, "put your lifejackets on!"

The parable takes a poetic turn at this point when it says, *"Now in the fourth watch of the night Jesus went to them, walking on the sea."* What does that mean? What is the *fourth watch*?

The fourth watch is late in the night. It's the hour that is the darkest before the dawn, the time when there is no time – the previous day is ended and the new day has not yet begun. If you wake up in the fourth watch you may lie in bed feeling like the smallest speck in the universe, overcome with emptiness, unsure about things you felt sure of only hours before. You can feel lonely, alone and scared in the fourth watch.

But the fourth watch is also the time that change can happen. There are no rules in the fourth watch since this

The Mary Mind

is the time that slips between the cracks. The apostles are in this place – this time when either fear or revelation will take their lives.

Now put yourself in the boat. Remember, the apostles represent us in this dramatic parable, so climb into the boat to make it more personal. You have rowed out too far to turn back, but the journey ahead seems impossibly long and dangerous. This is now *your* fourth watch. This is your time of no time, when a spiritual door can open and you either run through it or slam it shut. This moment of change can feel like a boat thrown and tossed by the sea. It can look like death is coming for you.

The disciples did indeed think they saw death coming for them in the form of a ghost, *"and they cried out for fear."* But it was Jesus, the *Holy* Ghost, the Christ Consciousness, coming to make sure they made it *"to the other side."* Still, even when Jesus identifies himself, they can't believe it; they can't let go of The Joseph Mind.

It's at this point that Peter calls out to the apparition on the water. He needs proof, so he challenges Jesus to make it possible for him to also walk on the water. Peter steps out of the boat and walks toward Jesus. But when the wind picks up, Peter gets scared; he doubts the Truth and begins to sink. Of course Jesus reaches out to save his brother and brings him safely back to the boat, calming the nature of the sea and the nature of the disciple's fear.

Do you see yourself in this story? As you make your way through life you *will* come to the fourth watch and it *will* be your time of terror or change. The decision is yours. You may have to choose between *Truth* and *fact*, and it can feel like you're being pulled apart. The *facts* are familiar, they seem solid and sure, but you can't deny that you also hear another voice in the background. This is the voice of *Truth*. This voice can sometimes sound crazy, seem foolish and dangerous and appear to go against the nature of the world. But that voice is a call from The Mary Mind, and it only wants to help.

In the story, help appears in a form that does not look like help. In fact, it terrifies the disciples and they resist it. Has this also been true in your own story? When you've been in the fourth watch, unsure and scared, have you ever refused the rescue because it doesn't look like the help you prayed for? This is called missing the lifeboat because you won't jump off the sinking ship. It's this stubbornness that takes us to a bottom, then opens a trap door and takes us to a deeper bottom. We can't contemplate change or hold hands with transition. We won't even scoot over just a little to let a big shift happen.

That's what this miracle is about – the lack of willingness to change our mind. It's a parable about finding our way in the fourth watch, the timeless place where change happens. It's about the trip *"to the other side"* of our minds. From The Joseph Mind to The Mary Mind.

Crucifixion and Resurrection

Do you understand that your life is more than what you think it is, and less than what you believe it is?

A lot of religions get really possessive about the death of Jesus. It's an especially gruesome way to die and it would be really hard to watch. Yet you go into almost any Christian church and you'll find a statue, painting or stained glass window depicting the final agony of Jesus. It's a friendly reminder from the church that you are a guilty sinner and that nailing Jesus to a cross was the sacrifice needed to atone for your sins.

That's a heavy load, but if that's what someone wants to believe, we're not here to take it away from them. For millions of people the meaning of Jesus' death is non-negotiable and worth fighting for. But, we *are* going to offer you our thoughts on the topic because this is almost the end of the book and that's the kind of folks we are.

There is a lot of drama around the crucifixion. The days leading up to it, the night before, who did what, what was said, how he carried his own cross. So much meaning has been laid on all these ideas that it's impossible not to feel some kind of charge around the topic. And the resurrection is no different – there's lots of emotion packed into that one too. You really can't talk about the crucifixion without the resurrection. They go hand-in-hand. For the death of Jesus to make sense in this parable, you have to have both.

The Mary Mind

We've said, and the Bible says, that Jesus was a teacher. So as a teacher, what could he possibly be teaching us by dying up on that cross? Most Christian religions see the crucifixion as Jesus dying for *us*, for our sins. But guess what? We don't.

The four gospels walk you through the life of Jesus, from birth to death. *The Mary Mind* has taken that walk with you, but we've taken the road less traveled. At this point, if you have not thrown this book out the window, then we know you have the willingness and openness to find a deeper spiritual meaning in the final chapter of Jesus' life. If you can go this final mile with us, and see even his crucifixion in terms of a parable, then we can offer you a vision of life out of a story of death.

In this parable, Jesus the teacher is delivering his final lecture to us. In a way, he *is* dying for us, but his dying is not a sacrifice or atonement for our sins. He is showing us in a spectacular way the most famous killing in history – but it's not about his body. The crucifixion is the death of The Joseph Mind and everything that goes with it.

All the lessons that Jesus taught have brought us to this last exam, but most people have dropped the course by now. They think the crucifixion of The Joseph Mind is terrifying and means letting go of all the things they love and have worked for.

Again, we are not here to argue about or make light of the crucifixion. We're just offering a different way to think about it. We see it as the last gasp of the mind that thought Peace and Love was not the answer to everything.

The cross that holds Jesus is huge and heavy, with spikes that pass through his hands and feet. All four gospels, Matthew, Mark, Luke and John, describe the scene — the smugness of the soldiers and the sadness of loved ones gathered at the foot of the cross. While above them, Jesus bled to death.

Jesus the man is indeed dying. His earthly suit, the same one we all wear, is being ripped apart. His human being-ness is dissolving right before our eyes. How can we not see this as anything but Jesus' life slipping away?

The answer to that question is in Luke 23:46, NKJV, *"into your hands I commit my spirit."* Most people read that and see it as the final prayer of Jesus to his father in heaven. That makes sense, but if you sit with The Mary Mind, *"into your hands I commit my spirit,"* becomes the living message of the crucifixion, not the last will and testament.

Jesus speaks these words as his body lets go of its last breath. It's a devastating moment, if you take the moment literally. But we're looking at it as a parable, and parables are always more than they appear to be.

The crucifixion is loaded with centuries of religious dogma. Powerful institutions have been built around the idea of Jesus dying for us. We've been threatened with damning repercussions if we don't believe what we've been told to

The Mary Mind

believe. War, hate and millions of lives lost have been the result of this dogma. Where has the message of Peace and Love gone?

We have to find another way to see the crucifixion. It has to mean more than just an enormous threat to our afterlife. Would Jesus do that to us? If you believe anything about Jesus, believe that he would not forsake us at this point.

The crucifixion parable is not about Jesus dying. Yes, his body dies, but that is not the message here. Our teacher Jesus does not give up on us even as his body is giving up its life. He is now asking us one bonus question, *"Do you understand that your life is more than what you think it is, and less than what you believe it is?"*

This question wraps it up. Jesus is asking us if we see the *fact* and the *Truth* about our lives. The *fact* is that the only purpose of our life is to find the *Truth* about our life.

In a very dramatic way this parable's deepest meaning, *"into your hands I commit my spirit,"* is about making the transition from human being to spiritual being. The Joseph Mind melts away, taking our attachments to the gold, frankincense and myrrh we *thought* we loved. In its place, The Mary Mind opens up to what it *knows* is Love. The cross is Jesus' most dramatic lesson told in the most breathtaking way. But this is not the end of the story. There is still resurrection.

We began this book with Mary and we will end this book with Mary. Jesus has been our teacher, but Mary has been our ideal. When she was visited by the angel, her mind opened up to Love in a quiet moment of revelation. She knew the *Truth of life* and left the *facts of life* behind. In her own way, she crucified herself when she said, *"Yes."* She gave up *who* she was and committed her spirit to *what* she was – pure Christ Consciousness. Like the crucifixion, the resurrection is not about the body. It is the birth of The Mind of Peace, The Holy Mind, The Mind of Love.

Every miracle we have looked at has been a parable about crucifixion and resurrection.

The cross is the symbol of letting go of The Joseph Mind. The resurrection is the symbol of the awakening Mary Mind, which leads us to the Awareness of the Christ Consciousness and the Enlightenment that remembers to choose Peace. Forever and ever.

Benediction

If you feel like the religion built up around Jesus has become political, divisive and even violent, you're not alone. Jesus and his message of Peace and Love have been driven out of the church, down a dead end road and kicked out of the car.

Religion now seems to be an "us" versus "them" war, with a jumbled set of ideas and rules that range from true good intentions to destructive mind control. The idea of a punishing God has broken us and filled us with guilt and fear – and religion has positioned itself to be the only way to save us from the guilt and fear that religion itself has created.

This has been religion's trump card – instilling fear in us if we dare to think for ourselves. Fear has taken control of our minds and our hearts. We've been raised on this fear for a very long time. It's what we know. It's almost in our DNA.

When we are brought up in fear we see threats everywhere we go. Differences become religious calls to war. Children grow up to hate and call it holy. And all this is somehow blessed in the name of Jesus and God. This is insane.

Any teaching, philosophy, dogma or belief that leaves us frightened about who we are, fearful of who others are, or terrified we're on our way to hell, is not a spiritual teaching. It may indeed be a religious teaching, but it is not spiritual and it has nothing to do with Jesus.

The only message Jesus taught was Peace and Love, which has somehow been turned into a script for judgment and conflict. How could the spiritual example that Jesus gave us be translated into the justification for war, hate, prejudice and persecution? How in the world has it come to this?

Jesus did not teach hate. He did not teach differences. He did not teach war. He did not teach religion. His mission was not to start something called Christianity. Jesus was one man, not a movement. He did not shout from a pulpit about your afterlife. He spoke about living in the here and now. Living as an example of Faith, Hope and Love. And the greatest of these is Love.

We've talked a lot about the *Christ Consciousness, Enlightenment,* and *Awakening.* Those are three big concepts and we think it would be irresponsible if we didn't wrap up with some thoughts about those ideas.

The co-authors have opened the church windows a little and let some light and air into the place. This gave us some breathing room and showed us where to start dropping our baggage of old beliefs and religious fears. Once that load was lightened, we walked around the place and kicked open the doors that have shut Jesus away and tried to hide his message of Peace and Love.

Now, it's your turn to open some windows. To do this, you'll need to drop some baggage and drive the fear out of your mind. Think of it as an exorcism, because fear has truly turned us into monsters. Fear confuses us into a mob mentality state of mind, tragically killing off:

The Mary Mind

1. *Self-introspection*
2. *Individual spiritual growth*
3. *A personal connection with Love, or God*

There you have three ways to think about those three big concepts of *Enlightenment, Awakening* and *Christ Consciousness:*

1. *Self-introspection* opens your mind to Enlightenment.
2. *Individual spiritual growth* walks you toward Awakening.
3. *A personal connection with Love* is your state of Christ Consciousness.

The Mary Mind is nothing more than the Mind that has decided fear does not work. Fear keeps a person small and their mind unable to think for itself. Fear installs pre-programmed beliefs. Fear is heavy and cold.

We've been skillfully trained by the enemies of Love to believe that all the names for fear – war, hate, borders, walls, weapons and power, just to name just a few – are signs of strength and sometimes even called "God's will." While all the names for Love – Compassion, Kindness, Charity, Goodwill, Helpfulness, Truth and Peace, just to name a few – are good topics for a Sunday sermon, but in actual practice are weak and won't get us what we want.

Choosing Peace goes against centuries of human behavior, cultural beliefs and political policy. But behavior, belief and policies can all be changed. They're usually not changed overnight, but they can be chipped away a day at a time, a thought at a time, a life at a time. And luckily, you don't have to change anybody's mind about all this. You just have to change *your* mind.

The gospels are a user's guide to this mind change. By walking us through the life of Jesus and showing us Mary's willingness to be filled with the Christ Consciousness, the four books give us an example to follow. To make this change, you start by asking yourself, *"What is the opposite of fear?"*

The answer is *Love*.

As we said in the beginning, the Love we're talking about is not romantic. It's also not something we can accurately describe with words. Descriptions are limited by the words we use, and the words we use are limited by things that have been described before. This creates a trap, where nothing new gets in.

The best way we know how to say it is that *Love is the result of a Mind at Peace*. A Mind at Peace is exactly what it sounds like – a mind that is not fighting. A mind without thoughts of conflict. A mind that has left behind all the justifications for pride, greed, lust, envy, gluttony, wrath and sloth. And to bring this understanding full circle, a Mind at Peace is a Mind that remembers all the names for Love – Compassion, Charity, Kindness, Helpfulness, and Truth. Just to name a few.

The Mary Mind

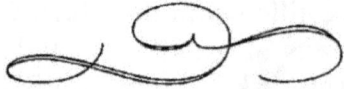

Jesus and Mary are our teachers, so every aspect and detail of their stories are lessons. When we see this, we can stop worshipping and start listening. Jesus and Mary step off the pages of the Bible and reach across time to walk with us.

The Mary Mind has offered you a new way to think about some very old stories. The gospels, seen as rich spiritual texts, can become an agent for change – if we take the fear out of them.

There is no fear in the message of Jesus.
Just Peace and Love.

www.ingramcontent.com/pod-product-compliance
Lightning Source LLC
LaVergne TN
LVHW041633070426
835507LV00008B/604